D0808683

ECHOES OF A VANISHED WORLD

ECHOES OF A VANISHED WORLD

A Traveller's Lifetime in Pictures

ROBIN HANBURY-TENISON

GARAGE PRESS 2012

This book has been designed & published by Graham Ovenden & Robin Hanbury-Tenison at the Garage Press 2012

Dedicated to all the tribal people who have shown me such kindness and hospitality throughout my travels; to Johnny Clements, who drove with me to Ceylon, to Richard Mason, with whom I crossed South America, to Hugh Dunphy, with whom I crossed Eastern Sulawesi and, above all to my late wife, Marika, who came with me on many expeditions in those long ago days.

Robin Hanbury-Tenison

Acknowledgements:
Grateful thanks to Thames & Hudson for there support and encouragement.
Also to John Langley and everyone at the National Theatre for arranging the eight week long exhibition of these photographs in the foyer of the Olivier Theatre, for which this book will also serve as the catalogue.

<Frontispiece: Indonesia 1973 Mentawai man by a waterfall on the Island of Siberut off the coast of Sumatra. Marika and I were the first outsiders to see this waterfall, which was up a long, rocky riverbed and was called Kulukubu. It fell in a white curtain shot with rainbows a sheer hundred feet into a deep pool of clear water, silencing the tropical din with its rushing and wetting the surrounding vegetation with spray. There is a legend that two women were fishing at the top and one fell near the edge. The other went to help her and both were swept over and drowned. Now sometimes their hands are seen above the water in the pool, a bad omen foretelling disaster.

ISBN 978-0-9566803-2-7

Copyright   Robin Hanbury-Tenison   2012
Garage Press

LANDSCAPES OF THE HEART

I was ten years old I when wrote my first book; sixteen pages long and fancifully illustrated, entitled *Jungle Warriors of the Forbidden City*. It was mostly drawn from the stories of Rider Haggard and Edgar Rice Burroughs, as well as the stack of *National Geographic* magazines that my grandfather kept under his bed, and which, for mysterious reasons, I was not supposed to read. My grandfather – a coal miner from Yorkshire - had never been abroad, and yet he was filled with enthusiasm for stories of distant places - cannibal tribes; Arctic landscapes; islands; explorers - and though he was barely literate himself, encouraged me to read, to write and to discover as much as I could of the world. At the time, that wasn't much. But *stories are roads*, he used to say, *that can lead you anywhere*, and as it happened, stories have led me further than even my grandfather would have expected. But the best and most well-loved stories are those that reach across culture and time to reveal an essential humanity behind the exotic trappings; the landscape of shared memory; the geography of the human heart.

The story you see before you is one of these. Ostensibly an archive of photographs collected by one remarkable man on his travels to some of the world's most isolated communities, it is in fact a rich and complex series of stories, narrated, partly by the man himself in his clear, evocative prose, and partly by the people he has chosen to depict; tribal people from such varied locations as the rainforests of Sarawak, the outer islands of Indonesia and the wastes of the Sahara Desert.

Robin Hanbury-Tenison is a natural born storyteller. A founder of Survival International and rightly described as "the greatest explorer of the past 20 years" (*Sunday Times, 1982*), his images speak directly to us in a voice that is fresh and clear. There is nothing self-conscious or patronizing about his photographs, or his prose. Instead there is deep admiration, a sense of wonder, respect and a desire to share what he sees with a world that has grown increasingly out of touch with the things that really matter. My grandfather would have admired him, and recognized the essentials of his story as instinctively as I do myself. There is history here, and adventure, and excitement. *We took blowpipes and hunting dogs with us and lived off the land.* There is a real magic in such a phrase. Or: *The temples in Pagan had massive gold Buddhas reclining neglected in their dark interiors. Nothing much had changed in 700 years since Genghis Khan razed the city.* Surely this is the stuff of childhood fantasy. Just reading it makes the heart beat faster, the imagination soar. And yet, the author also allows his photographs to speak for themselves, directly to the public.

And how clearly they speak! One of the charms of these images is their spontaneity. Although he has an artist's eye, Robin Hanbury-Tenison is never just a spectator. Each photograph is a window to a different story, close enough to touch, the characters depicted with affection and a curious intimacy. Young men, jostling for the respect of their peers. Mothers with their children. Beautiful young people, as poised as catwalk models. Children playing, oblivious of anything but the game. There is life here, and death; drama and laughter; music and cooking and hunting and art. Most of all, there is that essential, magic ingredient that makes a story come to life; that sense of shared humanity; a story that all of us understand, and that runs through every story ever told.

Looking at these pictures, most of them taken in the '50s and '60s, of vanished places and ways of life that have since changed beyond recognition, the thing that strikes me most is how familiar they seem. A Penan hunter, aiming his blowpipe, machete stuck into the belt of his bark loincloth, displays exactly the same expression of intense concentration as a soldier with his rifle – he is even wearing camouflage; his arms and legs covered with painted designs that break up his silhouette. A classroom of young flautists, demonstrating their skills under the eye of their teacher – all intent on the music, except one little girl, who dares to look directly at the camera – thereby confirming everything we know about the curiosity of children worldwide. A father and son going fishing, the child carrying a tiny version of his father's long fishing pole. Apart from differences in location, race and clothing, these faces and communities might be from anywhere in the world, and that is an essential part of their charm, reminding us that whatever our perceived differences, we are all connected. Diverse as we may be, we share far more than we differ. And the fear of losing our way of life - eroded as it is on all sides by the pressures of modern living - is one that we can all understand, wherever we happen to be in the world.

This stunning archive is not just a portal into a series of vanished places. It is not just a collection of stories, or even just a memoir of an era of exploration. It is a reminder of what we share, as human beings, with the rest of the world. It is a reminder of our collective responsibility for what happens when we allow ourselves to lose our sense of wonder and involvement with those cultures once described as "primitive". This archive is an antidote to that kind of complacency. We have a great deal still to learn from tribal cultures, as we have only recently begun to find out. And, as my grandfather knew well, the best way to teach is through story. This marvellous story – the story of a man who went off in search of other worlds and brought them back for us to experience – has already taught me so much, and has once more fired my enthusiasm for distant places, distant times. I hope you enjoy his work as much as I have enjoyed it. I hope it makes you dream a little. And I hope that you will recognize something to be treasured here, and to be passed on to future generations.

JOANNE HARRIS

INTRODUCTION

Thanks to the genius of Graham Ovenden, some of my simple early photographs have been turned into works of art. For me, this has been a miracle, as I have never thought of myself primarily as a photographer. During my ridiculously extensive travels around the world, I have always concentrated on looking and learning and trying to understand. Indeed, in recent years I have often deliberately not taken a camera, since I found that the obsessive need to keep my eye glued to the viewfinder meant that I failed to observe what was happening, to listen to the sounds and absorb the atmosphere. The fact that I had a mass of images did not compensate me in retrospect for the loss of the experience. Nonetheless, back in those early days I often was in extraordinary places, which have now changed dramatically, and with people whose lives have been transformed, not always for the better, by modernity. I snapped away and I kept many of the negatives. Graham is kind enough to say that I have an eye for form and moment, but I want to make it crystal clear that 99% of any pleasure you may derive from these pictures comes from his extraordinary skill at making photographic silk purses out of amateur pig's ears rather than from any small talent I may have exercised when, fortuitously, I was in the right place at the right moment.

Robin Hanbury-Tenison

The perfect traveller's rucksack entirely hand made from nature's produce. Borneo 1958

In the summer of 1957, on coming down from Oxford, I set out from London in a battered World War II Jeep, which I bought for £100, to make the first overland drive to Ceylon (now Sri Lanka). The year before, a joint Oxford and Cambridge expedition in three brand new Landrovers had made the first overland drive from London to Singapore, a feat never since repeated, unlike mine, which has been done many times, becoming known as the hippy trail in the 1960s.

My companion was a delightful Irish neighbour, Johnny Lucas-Clements, who was fortunately a brilliant mechanic, as our Jeep was decrepit. After selling the wrecked remains in Colombo, I travelled alone by cargo boat, bus and train through Indo-China to Borneo, an island I have returned to many times since, on many expeditions.

On our way from London to Ceylon we wandered through Persia, Afghanistan and India. The earliest photographs which have survived begin here in Persepolis, where we camped among the ruins long before there were any guards or other visitors. Built by Darius and his son Xerxes during the 6th and 5th century BC, it was destroyed by Alexander the Great in 330 BC.   Persia 1957

Madurai, India. Sunday 8th December 1957. One of the Hindu temples at Madurai, possibly the oldest continually inhabited city in the world. In recent years, the temples have been covered in scaffolding, restored and painted. In 1957 they were partly overgrown and monkeys scrambled through the foliage.> India 1957

Mandalay. New Year's Day 1958. Mandalay town was founded and laid out by King Mindon in 1857, exactly a hundred years before I arrived there. The Palace was built at the same time, but in March 1945, when occupied by the Japanese, General Slim and the 14th army conducted a twelve day siege, during which almost the entire wooden building was destroyed. All that was left were the royal mint and a few watch towers surrounded by the moat. The crumbling red brick walls of the palace overlooked wide stretches of weed and water lily covered water, in which were reflected many and varied trees. Modern pictures show an ugly white concrete barrier along the water's edge. Burma 1958

< A moated palace somewhere near Madurai. India 1957

Pagan (now Bagan), Burma. Sunday 5th January 1958. On arrival at the deserted city, then called Pagan, but changed to Bagan in 1989 by the military junta, I hired a dog cart pulled by an old horse and travelled lazily around the ruins. The capital of the First Burmese Empire in the 11th to 13th centuries, when most of the temples were built, Pagan was laid waste by the Mongols in 1287, after the king refused to pay tribute to Kublai Khan. An earthquake on the 8th of July 1975 destroyed more than half the original 5000 temples and many of those which survived have been badly restored with modern materials by the junta, who have also built a golf course between them. Modern tourists see a very different and much diminished place to the utterly abandoned and peaceful wonderland I saw more than fifty years ago. Burma 1958

< I travelled from Mandalay to Pagan down the Irrawaddy on a noisy little paddle steamer. For my protection, I was locked in a cage on the prow, since the country was at that time over run by bandits, who were likely to come on board and rob everyone. I slept on the deck wrapped in a mosquito net. My diet was two tangerines and a mouthful of rice. a & b Burma 1958

A Pagan monk with freshly shaven head was one of the few people I met among the ruins.   Burma 1958

< There was an old mattress in the back of my horse-drawn carriage, on which I reclined, as my young driver dozed and the horse plodded on. Apart from a handful of monks in orange robes, I saw not another soul. Inside the temples were scary little stone stairways to the tops, from which I gazed on pristine views. Burma 1958

< Pagan view of temples and ox carts. Nothing much had changed in the 700 years since Kublai Khan razed the city in 1287.   Burma 1958

Many of the temples in Pagan had, in those days, massive gold Buddhas reclining neglected in their dark interiors.   Burma 1958

< The colossal sandstone seated Thandawgya Buddha was decapitated in the 1975 earthquake.This may well be the only surviving photograph of this Buddha's original head, which has been replaced with crude faceless blocks. Six meters tall, it was erected by King Narathihapate in 1284, three years before the Mongol invasion. Burma 1958

Angkor January 1958. I spent a week wandering alone through the ruins of Angkor, transported between temples in a pedal rickshaw. There was no hotel then, nor other tourists, and I lived in a house in Siem Reap. Once a week a twin-engined DC3 flew in from Bangkok and those on board were able to pay a quick visit before flying out again. I chose to stay. Although none of the subsequent restoration and tourist infrastructure was then in place, it was a wonderful time to gaze at the statues in solitude. Cambodia 1958

I left Siem Reap on the ferry which used to ply across the Tonle Sap, the enormous lake connected to the Mekong River, which plays a vital role in Cambodia's economy, being extraordinarily rich in fish. Today there is a bridge and the lake is threatened by highly controversial plans for hydroelectric dams. Cambodia 1958 >

The floating market 1958. Today many of Bangkok's canals have been filled in and some of those
that remain have become tourist sites. Thailand 1958

< View from a Bangkok window of a temple. Thailand 1958

Guano carrier. Today some guano is still collected, but now modern sacks are used.   Borneo 1958

< Two important products were being harvested from the Niah cave. The millions of bats produced vast quantities of guano, a valuable fertilizer, and this was carried down to the coast by the local Dyaks along slippery raised walkways. Each basket weighed up to 220 pounds (100 kilos). The many swiftlets, which also lived in the cave, made nests which were collected and sent to China, where they were greatly prized as food. The slim poles, up which the nest gatherers climbed, can be seen in the picture of the cave.   Borneo 1958

< Niah Cave, Sarawak, Borneo February 1958. I reached the Niah cave by boat and walked in from the coast, as there was no road there then. Tom Harrisson and Gathorne Medway (now the Earl of Cranbrook) were living in the cave excavating the then earliest prehistoric skull in the world: 40,000 year old Borneo Man, the oldest human remains in South East Asia. They were also studying the many bats and I was put to work dissecting bat lice. Borneo 1958

On the Tinjar River in Sarawak the girls used heavy brass weights to stretch their earlobes down to their shoulders. Today they have nearly all had them sewn up. This girl had put on her best blouse because we were visiting her longhouse with the Catholic bishop of Borneo on his annual tour. The longhouses along the banks of Sarawak's rivers were a delight to visit in those days. We would be welcomed with some bangs from ancient shotguns and then escorted up the slippery notched poles to the house by captivating bare breasted girls, who sang and chanted as they helped us not to fall. Borneo 1976

They start stretching the ears when very young. Borneo 1976 >

At the headwaters of the Tinjar I joined a group of Penan to cross the watershed between that river and the Belepeh River, a tributary of the Rejang. This journey had not been made since Tom Harrisson did it for the first time in 1932 while on an Oxford University Exploration Club expedition. This was one of the young Penan who accompanied me. He and his companions were supremely fit and revelled in the excuse to make the journey with me. We took blowpipes and hunting dogs with us and lived off the land. A network of rivulets and rocky stream beds took us through pristine forest. Borneo 1976

He had to leave his young wife for two weeks, which she was not happy about. Borneo 1976

The head man of the Penan group did not come with us. His headband is made of clouded leopard skin. In his ears are teeth which he insisted were from a tiger. Although tigers, as opposed to leopards, feature largely in Dyak and Penan folklore, there is no confirmed record of a tiger ever being seen in Borneo. Borneo 1958-1976

Penan with loincloth. This one is made of cloth, but most were then still made of bark. Borneo 1976 >

Here one of the older Penan who came with me is carrying everything needed for a long journey. Later, when I lived for fifteen months in the Mulu National Park, I was to make many long tours with my Penan friend Nyapun, whose equipment was similar. Borneo 1976

The Penan are extraordinarily skilled with blowpipes. Note the puffed cheek. Borneo 1976

One of my Penan companions making a temporary shelter. It rained most nights, usually starting in late afternoon, which meant that making camp was always a rush. However, the Penan can make a waterproof house in less than an hour. Borneo 1976

Penan mother and child. As nomadic people, moving every ten days or so in pursuit of wild pigs and sago to harvest, the bond between parents and children is exceptionally strong. Borneo 1976 >

THE SAHARA

During the 1960's I made several long solo journeys by camel through the mountains of the Central Sahara searching for prehistoric rock art, which I attempted to film. In 1966, on my third journey, I reached the Aïr Mountains in Northern Niger, a pristine, remote desert region, the heartland of the Tuareg people, to which I was able to return several times thirty years later, after the worst drought in living memory. Sadly, this region is once again closed to outsiders, as conflict has broken out, partly the result of the war in Libya.

A Hausa boy on the Niger River, which carves its way through the southern Sahara. I travelled from Gao to Timbuktu in Mali by paddle steamer. On my return I was thrown in gaol for having taken photographs but managed to escape to neighbouring Niger. Mali 1966

< Gao. November 1966. Songhai fishermen pole their dugouts through the reeds along the banks of the Niger river. Bouba took me through beds of blue, white and pink water lilies, whose seeds were being collected for food. Lotus eaters! Mali 1966

December 1966. Riding by camel through the Aïr mountains north of Iferouane in Niger, my Tuareg companion Arambé and I came on two sisters herding their goats many days from any settlement. They were drawing water with a leather bucket from a deep and ancient well. Niger 1966

The younger Tuareg girl seemed to me to be as elegant and poised as any Paris model. The simple stylishness of her dress and her graceful pose could be thought of as 'wasted on the desert air' and yet I find it comforting to know that unselfconscious beauty like this exists in the most unexpected places. Niger 1966

In another wadi we came on this young boy and his donkey. Tuareg children are extraordinarily self possessed and often spend many weeks alone herding their flocks. Nearly forty years later, I was to spend forty days and nights travelling again by camel alone through these mountains with Tuareg companions, seeking enlightenment. Niger 1966

The Hausa sous prefet of Agades invited me on a picnic far out in the Tenere desert. The Tuareg prepared a great feast of goat meat. The sous prefet brought quantities of whisky and many of the girls from the Agades brothel, some with their children. Niger 1966

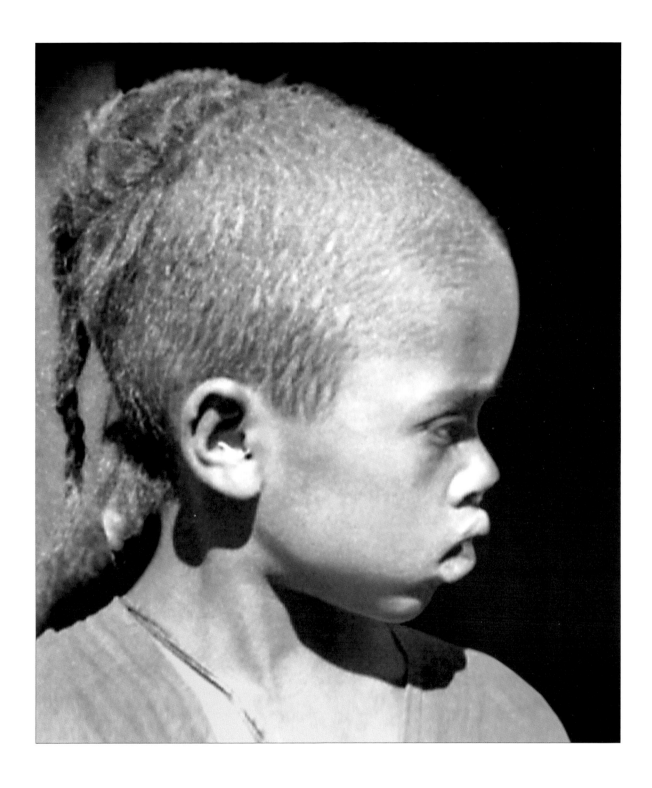

The children were cherished; their hair was braided and kohl was applied to their eyes. Niger 1966

Traditionally dyed with indigo and made from Sudanese cotton, many of the veils are blue, which gave
them their popular name: the Blue People of the Sahara. Niger 1966

When excited or amused, many of the women would ululate, making the extraordinary high pitched, quivering, tongue-fluttering shriek, which can be heard among indigenous people from Mexico to Bengal, but most of all in Africa. Niger 1966

Among the Tuareg the men are heavily veiled and never show their faces, unlike the women. Even when I travelled with them for many weeks, I never saw the mouths or noses of my older Tuareg companions. Niger 1966

In August 1969 I was in Fort Lamy, now called N'Djamena, the capital of Chad, organising the imminent arrival of an SRN6 Hovercraft. I was negotiating, as Deputy Leader of the Trans-Africa Hovercraft expedition, for permission to conduct trials on Lake Chad. Revolution was in the air, as usual in Chad, and groups of more than four people were banned, which made meetings difficult. However, the Minister of the Interior kindly invited me to tea and introduced me to two of his wives. Chad 1969

AMAZONAS

I reached the Americas in 1958 by working my passage on a Norwegian tramp steamer from Yokohama to Vancouver, across the North Pacific, before making my way down to Mexico. There I spent two months learning Spanish and visiting Aztec and Maya ruins. Later that same year, Richard Mason and I set off from Recife, the easternmost place in South America, to try and drive the first Brazilian made Jeep in as straight a line as possible across the continent at its widest point. For six months we hacked our way through the forest and built rafts when we came to tributaries of the Amazon. We covered some 6000 miles (10,000 kilometres), of which more than half had not previously been visited with a vehicle. With hindsight, I am not particularly proud of this exploit, as the subsequent Trans Amazonica highways have caused such devastation. But it brought us in contact with many Indian groups for the first time and my passion for their welfare was born. Three years later, Richard was ambushed and killed by uncontacted Indians while on an expedition to the source of the Iriri River with our mutual best friend from Oxford, John Hemming.

Subsequently, I was to make the first river crossing of the continent from North to South, from the mouth of the Orinoco to the River Plate. In 1971, I was invited by the Brazilian government to visit thirty-three Indian tribes and write the first report on their condition as Chairman of the newly created Survival International.

In 1958, while making the first land crossing of South America at its widest point with Richard Mason, we reached the island of Bananal on the Araguaia river. The Karaja Indian shamans were conducting a ceremony, which we were allowed to watch. They moved in two pairs, long grass skirts falling from below their arms and curtains of black grass swaying from high hats, hiding their faces completely and giving them the stature of giants. They shook black rattles and walked with short steps, bowing from side to side. Brazil 1958

A beautiful young Karaja girl taking part in an initiation ceremony. Wearing only a narrow leather apron, beads, arm and leg bands and painted with elaborate designs, she danced slowly backwards in front of the shamans, her eyes modestly cast down. Brazil 1958

Karaja men staring me down. Children of both sexes used to have two circles tattooed on their cheeks, called *omarura*. The cut was made with sharp fish teeth, after which a mixture of *genipa* and soot was rubbed in. Today adolescents just paint the circles during rituals. Macaws are also rare now, and protected, so that the elaborate feather headdresses we saw, and were often given, are now seldom seen. Brazil 1958

On the Rio dos Mortes we came on a group of barely contacted Xavante Indians. One of the men demonstrated how to use a bow and arrow – and where to keep a spare one! Brazil 1958

Xingu woman feeding parrot the proper way – just like its mother would. We saw many animals and birds kept by Indian communities and always cared for. They told us it was unthinkable to kill or eat any such pets, which were regarded as part of the family. Brazil 1971

< In 1971, on behalf of Survival International, I visited thirty three Brazilian Indian tribes during three months. Here a Gorotire (Kayapo) woman cradles a baby *coati mundi*, which she later breast fed with her own milk. Brazil 1971

A little boy with a fine feather headdresses. As parrots and macaws have become much rarer, this would be an unusual sight today. Brazil 1971

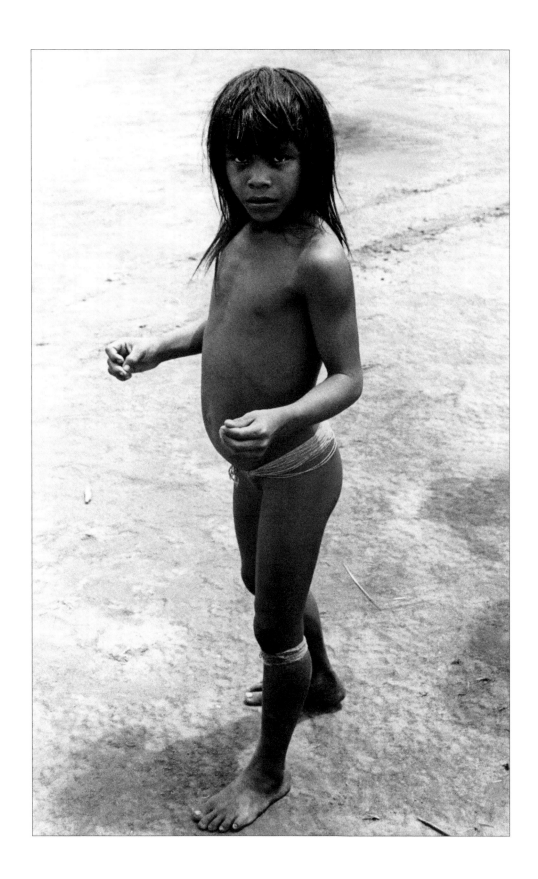

Nakedness is subjective. In the Xingu National Park, where the Villas Boas brothers had prevented access to missionaries and prospectors, most of the people did not bother with clothes. But this little girl would have felt bereft without her scant decorations. Brazil 1971

Xingu boys fighting, just as their elders did in more formal staged battles. Brazil 1971

< Indian mothers regularly breastfed their children until three or four years old, and
sometimes longer. Brazil 1971

< You are never too young to carry your baby brother. Brazil 1971

The chief of the Wauru, who are famous for their pottery, which was made by baking in an open fire. He may have been the last of his peoples' great craftsmen and here he shows two special pots he made for the Villas Boas brothers. Brazil 1971

< Yawalapeti Indians playing *jabui* flutes in the men's house in their village inside the Xingu Park. Brazil 1971

Behind a screen of plaited palm leaves, a Waura girl was living in isolation, having reached puberty. Secluded from the men of the tribe, she was learning the art of womanhood. Brazil 1971

Metal pots were among the few Western objects we saw being used in the Xingu National Park, apart from steel machetes and radios to communicate with the outside world. Here woman and children return from the river in the evening carrying water. Brazil 1971 >

Kamayura fisherman and son returning from the lagoon with his fish traps. Life is good. Brazil 1971 >

63

The Suya had only been contacted ten years before by the Villas Boas brothers. They had been contacted by the Villas Boas brothers in 1960, still isolated from other tribes, but dying in great numbers from flu, which had recently been introduced. Now, having come into the Xingu Park, they were on the increase again. Brazil 1971

At Diauarum in the north of the Xingu Park a Mentuktire man expressed anger at the news of a road which was proposed across his territory. Traditionally, men of the Kayapo group of Indians wore discs in their lower lip. Young boys would have their lips pierced and a wooden disc inserted, which was gradually increased in size. Brazil 1971 >

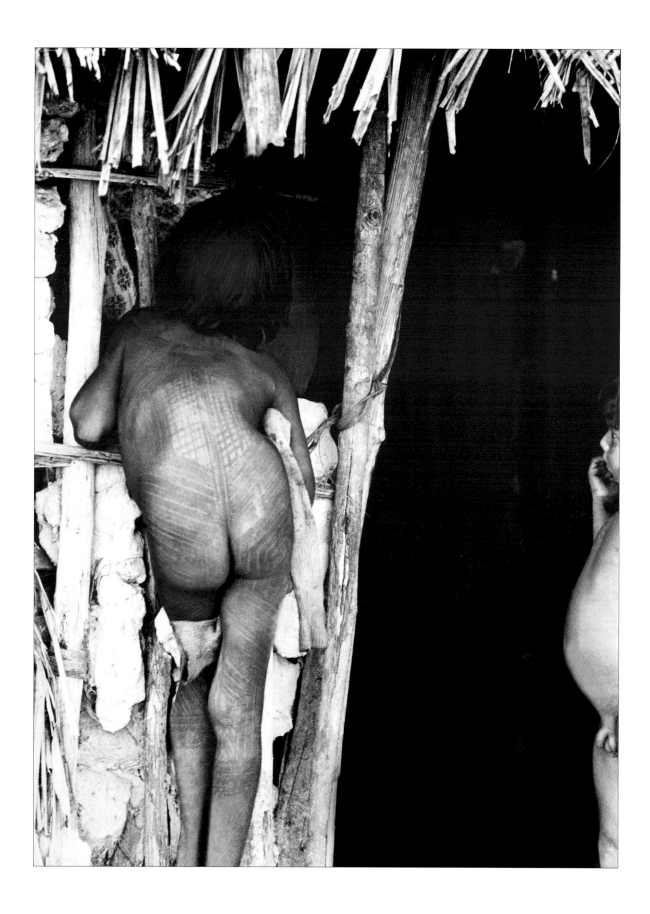

The Mentuktire, also called Txukarramai, living at Posto Leonardo inside the Xingu National Park are part of the Ge speaking northern Kayapo. A hunting and gathering people living along the Xingu River, they were first contacted by Karl von Steinen's expedition in the 1880s, but have continued to be fiercely independent until the present. About half the men had wooden discs in their lower lips. These were about four inches across and often stretched as thin as an elastic band. I could never understand how, in the rough and often hostile world they lived in, they could manage to go through life without splitting this narrow strip. The generally accepted reason for it was that it makes them look frightening and fierce to their enemies. Brazil 1971

< Body painting is usually done with *genipa* juice, which stains the skin black and lasts for about a fortnight. Brazil 1971

Xingu girls at Posto Leonardo watching the men dancing. Brazil 1971

< Xingu child running through tall grass. Brazil 1971

The great French anthropologist, Claude Lévi-Strauss, author of Tristes Tropiques, who was a firm supporter of Survival International until his death in 2009, lived with the Bororo tribe in Mato Grosso state in the 1930s. When we visited them in 1971 they were recovering from a confusing time, when protestant missionaries had forbidden traditional practices, such as decorating their bodies with feathers. This little girl shows the conflict of cultures. Brazil 1971

The Nambiquara, who lived in the Guaporé Valley near the Bolivian border, are different from other Brazilian tribes. Their language is tonal and they do not use hammocks, preferring to sleep in the ashes of their fires. Brazil 1971

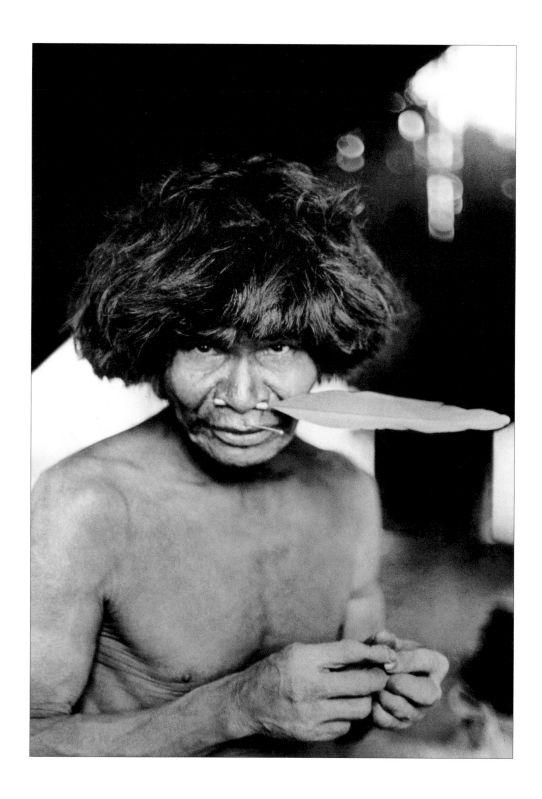

The Nambiquara are also unique in using a particular form of nose flute. This man has both a perforated upper lip and septum, through which he has put a macaw feather. Brazil 1971

Cattle rancher with big horn. These people were just arriving on Indian lands in the 50s, 60s and 70s. Nearly half the deforestation of the Brazilian Amazon has been caused by large scale cattle ranching. Today soya bean production poses the greatest threat to both the environment and the Indians. Brazil 1971 >

INDONESIA

Following publication of my Report and book on the Indians of Brazil, and in order to broaden the outreach of Survival's work, my first wife, Marika, and I made an extensive journey through Indonesia, visiting many of the isolated peoples of the Outer Islands and assessing their condition. I found some surprising similarities both in the size and diversity of both countries and their indigenous inhabitants, as well as the problems they faced, and continue to face. Each country covered a similar area of the earth's surface, albeit in Indonesia's case it was mostly sea, and had a population then of something over a hundred million. In the last forty years both have just about doubled the number of their inhabitants, while much of their rainforest has been cut down, bringing devastation to those who traditionally lived in them.

A Mentawai warrior. It takes a real man to wear flowers in your ears. Indonesia 1973

On our way up the Sabirut river we came on these strangely dressed girls. They had hurriedly put on grass skirts because they thought we might be the nuns, who had recently established a mission on the island. When they discovered we were not, they nearly died laughing. Indonesia 1973 >

The girls looked shocked when we came round the corner. Indonesia 1973 >

Little girl in the Borneo forest, as at home as any western child in a playground. Indonesia 1973

Ot Danum girl behind her longhouse on the Melawi River, Kalimantan. Indonesia 1973 >

Hats, which are made of nipah palm leaves, are often highly decorated with sea shells and beads, but their main function is protection against the sun and rain. Indonesia 1973

< Mother and son. Indonesia 1973

This basket weaver's hands and face reflect the fine quality of her work. Indonesia 1973

What are friends for? The women picked lice from each others heads as one sat and another knelt behind,
sifting with well-practiced fingers through the heavy tresses. Indonesia 1973 >

When water has to be carried a long way, bamboo tubes are used. Full, these are very heavy. Indonesia 1973

Bamboo pipes carry water through the forest to the village. Indonesia 1973

Pounding rice is hard work. The steady thumping is a constant background noise in longhouses. Indonesia 1973

Once pounded, it is flicked onto tightly woven matting. Indonesia 1973

< Then it is winnowed to remove the chaff. Indonesia 1973

The elegant swineherds. Five days journey up the Melawi river in Kalimantan, and far from so-called civilization, and yet these women are as elegant as if they were going to a ball. Indonesia 1973

Another modish farmer's wife. Indonesia 1973 >

The Universal chidhood gaze. Indonesia 1974

A To Wana girl in Eastern Sulawesi with big eyes and a frown. Indonesia 1974

A Smart umbrella in the middle of nowhere Indonesia 1973

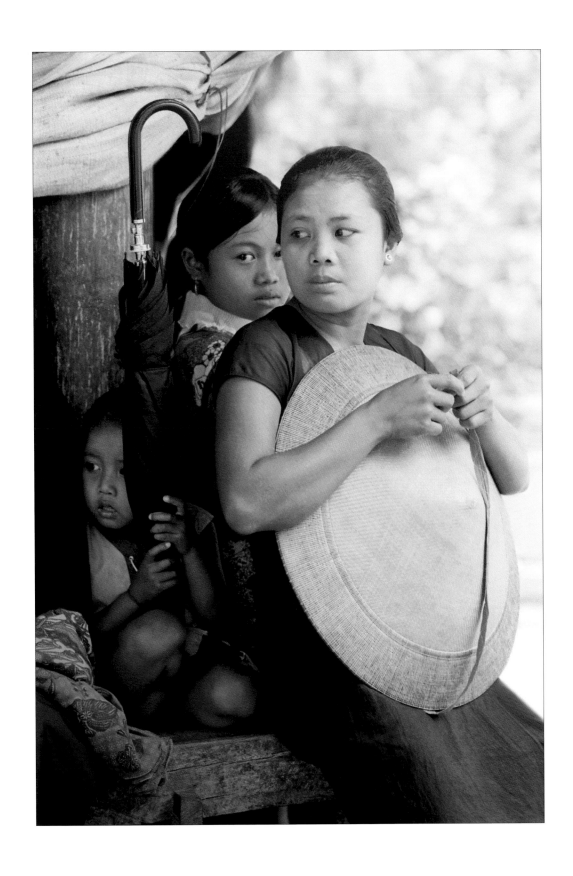

Watching me watching you. Indonesia 1973

A Toradja funeral in Sulawesi is the most elaborate and expensive event in their culture. We were lucky to witness one at which a buffalo was slaughtered before the corpse was carried to a cave in a nearby cliff. The body lay on a simple bier of bamboo like a large, trim bolster, neatly packaged in a carefully sewn-up striped cloth. A soft khaki hat, which had obviously belonged to the deceased, was hung over one end. Bodies of the dead lie in state inside Toraja houses for anything from three months to a year, the corpse tightly encased in many yards of coloured cloth, neatly sealed. Ritual mourning takes place every day while the body remains in the house and sacrifices are made at intervals during the interment. At the end the funeral is a fantastic affair attended by everyone who had contact or dealings in any way with the dead man. Mourners come from great distances to join in the feasting, to pay their respects, and to receive their rights. Seven men went to stand in a semi-circle around the body. They began to dance, singing as they did so, stamping back and forth, raising one leg after another and swaying from side to side. Indonesia 1973

A Toradja woman chewing betel at the funeral. Areca (<u>Areca catechu</u>) nuts have been chewed with betel leaves for thousands of years. It is a stimulant and freshens the breath, as well as staining the lips and teeth bright red. Leaves are continuously plucked from pouches or from a bundle kept on the head, lime is pounded and slivers of brown nut are cut off in the ritual of making small parcels, which are chewed and finally spat out in a neatly directed stream of scarlet juice. Indonesia 1973

High in the hills above the Toradja funeral we heard enchanting flute music in the distance. It was the haunting, floating, lighter-than-air music of pipes, thin but swelling, filling the plateau, filling the valley below, obscured by mist, and spreading out over the mountains. Soft music, the music of Pan, unforgettable, pure, fluting mountain sounds. We tracked down a small school where some forty children were playing a variety of bamboo wind instruments under the instruction of their teacher, who tapped out the rhythm on a blackboard. Most of the boys, ranging from teenagers to little tackers of no more than four or five, had unusual double pipes, which some were able to blow into two at a time. These seem to be unique to the Toradja. They were accompanied by a row of girls with high pitched flutes and a virtuoso older boy who played the melody, also on a flute. The result was a delightfully harmonic, haunting Alpine music. In the bare wooden classroom children of all ages were playing the strange instruments made from a network of bamboo stems painted white with black tops. They stopped to stare, round-eyed, and then continued playing as the teacher sharply rapped the blackboard covered with simple notes. 'Would you like to hear more?' he asked, and when we nodded he waved a baton at the children and they began a different tune, this time a happy 'umpah, umpah' beat, reminiscent of a brass band. The children's enthusiasm for the music was catching; they puffed their cheeks and put their hearts into it, the more sophisticated teenagers at the back blowing complicated tonal chords on the larger pipes and small children sitting on benches in the front row keeping pace with high, reedy sounds from simpler flutes. Indonesia 1973

< A graceful water carrier and her child. Indonesia 1973

The Dani farm rich gardens of sweet potato hidden in the western highlands of the Indonesian part of the island of New Guinea. The existence of the remote Baliem valley, the centre of their culture, only became known to the outside world in 1938, when the American zoologist, Richard Archbold, sighted rectangular fields below from his Caatalina flying boat. Indonesia 1973

Dani father and son. The men can be loving fathers, but with young children this may be strengthened by the custom that a man may not sleep with his wife until her last child can walk. Indonesia 1973

Dani woman eating sweet potato with a mutilated hand. Traditionally, a Dani woman will cut off the whole or part of her fingers whenever a husband, child or loved relation dies. As a result, the men are often better equipped at weaving baskets and nets, plaiting ropes and making necklaces. Indonesia 1973

Dani women always carried a woven net called *noken* across their backs, and had very short skirts, which we were told were woven from orchid fibres. Indonesia 1973

Asmat evening river scene. In 1973 there were thought to be about forty thousand Asmat people living in tidal mangrove swamps and lowland rain forests of southern Indonesian New Guinea. Well over half the tribe had by then been contacted and settled in villages on rivers near the coast, but many still lived in the interior and were much feared due to their reputation for cannibalism and headhunting. The land is regularly flooded and they are superb canoeists. Indonesia 1973

The Asmat people are famous for their fine carving, especially the towering *bis* poles made for funeral feasts. The finest collection of these is in the Metropolitan Museum of Art in New York and includes those collected by Michael Rockefeller. He had disappeared dramatically a decade after his boat capsized off the nearby coast and his body was never found. Here a woman is holding a freshly carved prow for a dugout canoe. Indonesia 1973 >

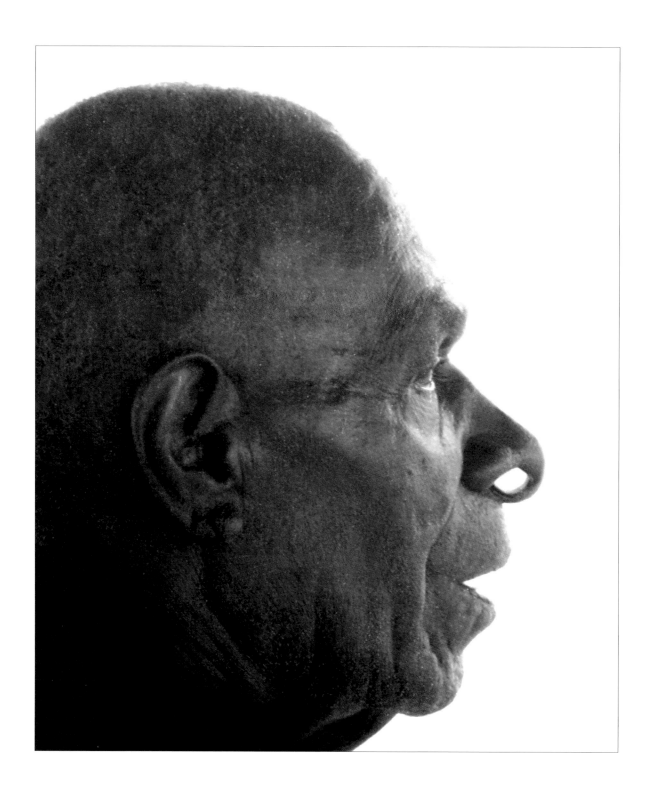

All Asmat man had perforated septums, a custom as common throughout the world as ear and lower lip piercing. Pig's tusks or a large bone through the nose are believed to give the face a fierce appearance. The bone is usually made from the leg bone of a pig, but some were then still made from the Tibia of an enemy slain in battle. Indonesia 1973

Nostril piercing was less common, but it enhances this handsome man's looks. Indonesia 1973 >

Two families lived in a miniature thatched communal house high on a cliff, into which they welcomed us, lighting tapers laced with *damar* gum which exuded a wonderful smell and were attached to the walls, giving their house the feel of a baronial hall. They fed us on boiled pumpkin, wild rice, little mud fish and river prawns cooked in hollow bamboo tubes. A tiny multicoloured parrot flew from shoulder to shoulder to peer at me inquisitively, while a small tame monkey searched for fleas in my hair. It seemed like paradise and we were reluctant to leave, but when we did so we felt sure that our passing had hardly affected their lives. Indonesia 1974

< In 1974 I walked with a friend across Eastern Sulawesi, travelling with the To Wana people. As we neared the northern coast, we came upon an apparently unknown group called the Kohumamao. Our host had an unusual spear and shield, which seemed more for defence than hunting, and yet I have never met gentler people. He built a raft on which I floated down the river to the coast. Indonesia 1974

This close protective relationship between children is a model for all societies. Indonesia 1973

This little girl displays a fabulous neckless made up of monkey teeth and coins amongst other decorative pieces. Indonesia 1973 >

Maya temple at Copan. The Maya were the greatest of all Mesoamerican civilizations, reaching their highest state of development between 250 and 900 AD. The Maya believed that the universe was constantly being created and destroyed in a never ending cycle, an idea being echoed today at the cutting edge of research into space. Some of the calculations now being deciphered from the stelea indicate a distinction between contemporary time and 'deep time'. There are calendars which seem to be dealing with cycles of millions, even billions, of years. Their incredibly complex Long Count calendar is still not fully understood. Its year dot, like the Christian 1st of January, year zero, is 11th August 3114 B.C. This was what the Maya thought of as the date when the current world began, the founding of the current universe. It is only about a thousand years later than the rather arbitrary date of 4004 BC calculated by Archbishop Ussher in 1650 as the moment when God created the Garden of Eden. The long Count calendar has a cycle of 1,872,000 days, which is just over 5000 years. The cycle ends on 21st December 2012, which some believe will be the end of the world. Or perhaps Armageddon in the form of a great flood, earthquake or other cataclysm will annihilate our corrupt society, which will then start a new and more perfect world. Some might say not before time. Guatemala 1972

< Communal family life teaches responsibility at an early age. Indonesia 1973

As lessons are learned about the dangers of rapid change and ill-conceived tampering with fragile ecosystems, as the energy crisis grows and the raw materials necessary for an expanding industrial society shrink, it may be that we will go cap in hand to seek the remaining self sufficient societies and ask their advice. It will be ironic if, when we do so, we find that they no longer exist, for they are the yeast in the bread of humanity.

Robin Hanbury-Tenison is President of SURVIVAL INTERNATIONAL, the movement for tribal peoples. Survival is the only organization working for tribal peoples' rights worldwide.

We work with hundreds of tribal communities and organizations. We are funded almost entirely by concerned members of the public and some foundations. We will not take national government money, because governments are the main violators of tribal peoples' rights, nor will we take money from companies which might be abusing tribal peoples.

About 250,000 supporters from nearly 100 countries have helped us financially; millions now routinely seek our information, published in seven languages. We never restrict our information or materials only to those who can pay. We want everyone to know about tribal peoples. www.survivalinternational.org

International Office:

Survial International
6 Charterhouse Buildings
London
EC1M 7ET
United Kingdom

T +44 (0)207 687 8700
F +44 (0)207 687 8701

info@survivalinternational.org

Overeseas offices:

USA:
Survival International USA
2325 3rd Street, Suite 401
San Francisco
CA 94107
USA

T (+1) 415-503-1254

info.usa@survivalinternational.org

ITALY:
Survival International Italia
Via Morigi 8
20123 Milano
Italy

T (+39) 02 890 0671
F (+39) 02 890 0674

info@survival.it

SPAIN:
Survival International Espana
Calle Principe, 12, 3
28012 - Madrid
Spain

T +34 91 521 7283
F +34 91523 1420

info@survival.es

FRANCE:
Survival International France
18 Rue Ernest et Henri Rousselle
75013 Paris
France

T +33 (0)1 4241 4762

info@survivalfrance.org

NETHERLANDS:
Survival International Netherlands
Van der Duynstrat 71
1051 AT Ansterdam
The Netherlands

T +31 (0)20 6860850

info@survivalinternational.nl

GERMANY:
Survival International Deutschland
Haus der Demokratie und Menschenrechte
Grefswalderstr.4
10405 Berlin
Deutschland

T +49 (0)30 72 29 31 08
F +49 (0)30 72 29 73 22

info@survivalinternational.de

AFTERWORD

Robin Hanbury-Tenison and I have been good friends and neighbours for some forty years. During this period I have been aware that he has photographed extensively while on his travels: his many books give evidence of his wide cultural and visual interests in these matters. However it was only when I had shown Robin my recent publications from Garage Press and suggested to him that there might be sufficient material of quality taken from his personal archive to make a book devoted largely to his photographic work, that this exciting project developed. Robin's foreword to this volume expresses his sentiments and modesty on the subject in hand, but I think both he and I must confess to our delight and in Robin's case, surprise, at the quality and quantity of the works unearthed. Many of the images reproduced within had not been looked at for fifty years! For me it is not only the natural structural rightness of his "camera eye" which gives aesthetic satisfaction, but most importantly, the communication of a deeply felt humanity for his fellow beings. After all, the reason for the existence of any art discipline is just that and Robin's *Lost Edens* prove a most eloquent validity of this.

Graham Ovenden

Index to the contents of this book

Signed copies of these photographs, taken as direct scans from the original negatives held by the Hanbury-Tenison collection. are available for purchase.

For further information please contact:

Nicky Akehurst at na@nickyakehurst.com

www.akehurstcreativemanagement.com